COLONIAL PEOPLE

The Gunsmith

WIL MARA

Cavendish Square

New York

Published in 2014 by Cavendish Square Publishing, LLC
303 Park Avenue South, Suite 1247, New York, NY 10010

Website: cavendishsq.com

This publication represents the opinions and views of the author based on his or her personal experience, knowledge, and research. The information in this book serves as a general guide only. The author and publisher have used their best efforts in preparing this book and disclaim liability rising directly or indirectly from the use and application of this book.

CPSIA Compliance Information: Batch #WS13CSQ

All websites were available and accurate when this book was sent to press.

Library of Congress Cataloging-in-Publication Data

Mara, Wil.
The gunsmith / Wil Mara.
p. cm. — (Colonial people)
Includes bibliographical references and index.
Summary: "Explores the life of a colonial gunsmith and his importance to the community, as well as everyday life responsibilities, and social practices during that time"—Provided by publisher.
ISBN 978-1-60870-414-9 (hardcover) — ISBN 978-1-62712-046-3 (paperback) — ISBN 978-1-60870-985-4 (ebook)
1. Gunsmiths—United States—History—17th century—Juvenile literature. 2. Gunsmiths—United States—History—18th century—Juvenile literature. 3. Gunsmithing—United States—History—17th century—Juvenile literature. 4. Gunsmithing—United States—History—18th century—Juvenile literature. 5. United States—Social life and customs—To 1775—Juvenile literature. 6. United States—History—Colonial period, ca. 1600-1775—Juvenile literature. I. Title. II. Series.
TS533.2.M36 2013
683.400973—dc23
2011028342

Editor: Peter Mavrikis
Art Director: Anahid Hamparian
Series Designer: Kay Petronio

Photo research by Marybeth Kavanagh

Cover photo by North Wind Picture Archives

The photographs in this book are used by permission and through the courtesy of: *North Wind Picture Archives*: 4, 8, 26, 40; *Alamy*: Patrick Ray Dunn, 32; *The Colonial Williamsburg Foundation*: 11, 13, 16, 17, 23, 34, 38

Printed in the United States of America

CONTENTS

ONE

Gunsmithing in the American Colonies

The early to mid-1600s saw masses of Europeans leave their homeland and cross the Atlantic in the hope of finding a better life in what would become the United States of America. Some were tired of the "class system" through which anyone who had not been born into a wealthy family had little chance of moving up society's ladder and enjoying the rewards of prosperity. Others left for religious reasons—specifically, they wished to practice beliefs that were not in keeping with the views of their country's religious establishment. A minority were wealthy people who used their money to purchase vast tracts of land and established plantations farmed by **indentured servants**, slaves, and renters.

These early European colonists knew all too well how difficult it would be to fulfill their dream. The sailing journey from Europe to America alone was fraught with peril. Wooden ships

Those who came to America from Europe in search of a better life relied on guns for their survival.

were unreliable in harsh weather, and many sank before reaching their destination. Sickness was another problem. If a few people became ill during the trip, the illness would spread quickly. There were few effective medications in those days, and a simple fever could turn deadly. This was also the age before the development of vaccines for devastating diseases such as smallpox, which had already killed millions around the world.

Those who were lucky enough to reach America in the 1600s realized that more challenges awaited. In the Chesapeake colonies, most arrivals were young, unmarried indentured men who worked on plantations. In New England, colonists tended to arrive in families and had enough money to purchase small plots of land. In order to eat, they had to become hunters and farmers. And in order to survive harsh weather, they had to build their own homes. Clearing land for farming and building shelter from raw timber was brutally hard work. Chopping a tree down with an ax or pulling a stump out of the ground was exhausting for even the most able-bodied individual. Once a colonial family built their home and tilled their fields, they still had to worry about attacks from wild animals or American Indians. Many American Indians were unhappy that they were being forced to share land that had previously been their exclusive domain.

Early American Gunsmithing

To meet the challenges of hunting wildlife and fending off enemies, guns were a necessity. In the earliest colonial days, hunting was the only way to secure live game. A colonist with a reliable rifle and a steady hand could go after beasts of all sizes—from deer and bear to squirrels, rabbits, muskrats, geese, ducks, and turkeys. Animals also provided value through their fur, feathers, teeth, and bones, all of which could be made into useful items. It would have been very difficult to catch any of these creatures without the aid of a firearm—and it would have been impossible to get firearms without the talents of the gunsmith.

Not every colonist had a gun. Crafting one from scratch or having one cleaned or repaired could be very expensive, and many colonists arrived in America with little or no money to spare. In some circumstances, colonial governments gave guns to ordinary people so they could fight in local **militias** or take part in larger conflicts. In both the Chesapeake area and New England, colonial governments made war on Indian tribes who refused to relinquish their land on English terms. English colonial governments also traded guns to Indians who agreed to fight their French, Dutch, and Spanish enemies. These four empires fought numerous wars in the 1600s and 1700s to take

A Jack of All Trades

It was not unusual for a gunsmith to be a master of several trades at the same time. Gunsmithing work was often taken up by blacksmiths, whitesmiths, armorers, cutlers, jewelers, cabinetmakers, and others. Some of these people built guns, whereas others just repaired or cleaned them. They might specialize in certain parts of a gun. For example, the cabinetmaker might be able to replace a broken stock but did not have the tools or skills to replace a damaged barrel. For a few, gunsmithing became a full-time profession. For others, it was purely a sideline occupation. One such multitalented smith was John Armstrong of Maryland, who produced guns of the highest quality, but was known particularly for his excellent woodcarving, silver inlays, and metalwork on the locks. Daniel Border, of Bedford Township in Pennsylvania, worked as a silversmith when he was not producing and maintaining guns. And Jacob Brant, a resident of Uniontown, Pennsylvania, did gunsmithing as a supplement to his work as a dealer in real estate.

Most gunsmiths had expertise in other trades as well. For some, gunsmithing was only a part-time profession.

control of North America, its people, and its resources.

The Fight for North America

Even during times of conflict, many gunsmiths did more repair and assembly work than actual gun creation. The real smiths were back in Europe, making gun parts and then shipping them to America. Once there, American smiths simply put the guns together. Also, European governments were not eager to supply colonists with weaponry and ammunition in the first place. Colonists who owned guns were colonists who had power, and that made them harder to control. "No more than necessary" seemed to be the rule in Europe concerning how many guns were put into colonists' hands.

As tensions between the British colonists and the French and French-allied Indians steadily grew in the mid-1700s, the demand for gunsmithing grew, too. It exploded after the French and Indian War (which began in 1754) with a rise in gun ownership, and by 1774, as tensions between the colonists and the British government increased.

The dawn of the **American Revolution** also launched the beginning of a very busy period in the craft of American gunsmithing. Whereas a smith might have made only one or two weapons a week previously, he was now being asked to produce a dozen or more. This meant hiring more men, gathering more raw materials, and sometimes even opening and managing small factories. Along with the making of guns came the responsibility of maintaining and repairing stores of them for the budding Revolutionary armies.

Of particular importance during this period was the Pennsylvania long rifle. It was first developed by German immigrants in the early 1600s, and by the mid-1700s it had evolved into a weapon of remarkable efficiency and high reputation throughout the American frontier. It became popular with Revolutionary soldiers, not only for its reliability but for its relative ease of manufacture and maintenance. Thus, the colonial gunsmiths who produced the long rifle and other weaponry played a crucial role not just in the arming of the colonists, but also in the contest for North America that resulted in the birth of a new nation—the United States of America. With this in mind, their importance in colonial history cannot be underestimated.

Gunsmiths became particularly important to American colonists during the American Revolution, when weapons, ammunition, and other accessories were in great demand.

TWO

The Colonial Gunsmith

Gunsmithing was a challenging trade that few people undertook and even fewer truly mastered. It required a combination of exacting manual skills, extreme patience and discipline, and a strong attention to detail. It took many years of practice and experience to become a gunsmith, and those who did often found themselves in high demand.

An Uncommon Tradesman

Smiths who came to America from England often found so little work that they went into other trades instead. Some became blacksmiths or jewelers, where they could use many of the same skills. Others went into altogether different professions, like farming or candlemaking. This often caused deep concern among government officials, who feared there would not be enough gunsmiths if there came a time when their talents were needed.

As a result, gunsmiths were often urged to stay in their original profession. Unfortunately, the smiths ignored such requests since business was so bad that they found it impossible to make a living. Officials then tried to sway the gunsmiths by offering tax breaks or outright payments. When this did not work either, governments often resorted to threatening gunsmiths with fines. Although this may have sent some smiths back to their shops (even if customers were hard to come by), they still had to take on other work.

Becoming a Gunsmith

Those who wished to learn the gunsmithing trade usually did so by first becoming **apprentices**. An apprentice was someone who agreed to work with an experienced gunsmith in order to learn and hopefully master the craft. Once a smith decided to take on an apprentice, a contract would be drawn up and signed by both sides.

Becoming a reputable gunsmith required years of study, practice, and hard work. Only the most skilled craftsmen mastered this difficult trade.

This was often done in a local courthouse, because it was considered an official legal document. If one person failed to live up to his obligations, the other could then go to the authorities and complain. This did happen from time to time. There are court records of apprentices complaining about masters who became lazy in their teaching duties. On the other hand, there are also records of masters offering rewards for apprentices who had run away. Fortunately, these instances were the exception rather than the rule.

As part of the initial agreement, the gunsmith was often obligated to give the apprentice a place to live, food, clothing, and sometimes a little money, as well as training in subjects such as literacy and arithmetic—skills needed to run a shop. The master also typically agreed to provide religious instruction or enforce church attendance. Most apprentices were in their early teens. Some were orphans or freed slaves whom local authorities placed with a smith in the hope of giving the youngster a start in life.

At the start of an apprenticeship, the young man would be given the simplest tasks to perform, such as cleaning the shop, routine tool maintenance, making fires in the **forge**, and so on. Gradually the master would then train the apprentice in work that was more challenging and required greater skill. The term of their apprenticeship normally lasted about three years, but this could vary tremendously depending upon the circumstances. Apprenticeships lasted longer during the earlier parts of the colonial period, and got shorter as tensions between America and Britain increased and the demand for weapons grew. Also, as the manufacture of guns evolved into a more assembly line-type style, apprentices might be taught only to specialize in one area of gunmaking, such as stocks or barrels. Thus, the apprentice period would be shorter than that of someone learning all aspects of gunsmithing. During and after the American Revolution, as demand for guns increased in America, this kind of specialization became more common.

At the end of an apprenticeship, the master was obligated to present his apprentice with certain "freedom dues." The master provided a signed document stating his confidence in his student's abilities. The apprentice might have to prove his skills by producing one reliable gun (or more) completely on his own. A master sometimes also provided the "graduate" with a set of basic smithing tools, a small amount of money, and even some new clothing. The apprentice would then move to another area as a "journeyman" to seek work in another master's shop until he had gained the money, the experience, and the reputation to be called a "master" and open a shop of his own. In some cases, an

A gunsmith had to be able to work with many different materials, including a variety of woods and metals.

Quality Control

In Europe, craftsmen were often required to join an organization known as a guild. Among its many other purposes, a guild worked to ensure that a certain level of quality was observed concerning the craft of its members. These high standards applied not only to gunsmiths but also to blacksmiths, silversmiths, goldsmiths, whitesmiths, and others. European guilds were often very specific in terms of what function of

A gunsmith's work had to be competent and reliable. Guns that did not work properly were not only useless, but also dangerous.

gunmaking each guild member performed. For example, there would be a guild for those who made only gun barrels, those who made locks, stocks, trigger guards, and so on.

Colonial America did not have a guild in the early days of gunsmithing. The only person who really got to judge the competency of a gunsmith's work was the customer who bought the rifle or pistol he made. Discovering that a gun was poor in quality often happened through an unfortunate accident, or through repeated failure to hit an intended target. It was also difficult to determine if a smith had any consistency in the quality of his work because guns were often made to a buyer's individual specifications.

This trend changed during the early to mid-1700s. As the new American government required a greater number of arms to be manufactured, it looked first to those gunsmiths whose work was most respected. Sometimes a gunsmith would receive government certification to reflect his competency and reliability.

apprentice developed a close friendship with his master, with the relationship becoming more like that between a father and son, and the apprentice was groomed to take over the master's shop.

The Skills Required

Perhaps the most remarkable aspect of the gunsmithing art was that the smith had to be skilled in many different areas. For example, he had to be able to work with a variety of materials, including different types of wood, common metals such as iron and steel, and more expensive metals such as brass, silver, and sometimes even gold. With these precious metals, a gunsmith had to be particularly careful with his work, since mistakes could be very costly.

The three main parts of a gun are the barrel, the stock, and the lock. When working with barrels, a gunsmith had to heat iron at extremely high temperatures before shaping the steel into long tubes. Most tubes were smooth-bored and were used in guns called muskets. Early muskets, called matchlocks, used a long fuse—the "match"—to ignite the powder and fire the weapon. By the late 1600s, smiths and users preferred "flintlocks" that used a steel hammer to strike a piece of flint to spark the powder. These muskets were quick to produce, but they fired accurately only at a range of much less than 100 yards. By the mid-1700s, gunsmiths from Germany who had come to Pennsylvania brought with them rifling technology that cut spiraled grooves on the inside of an elongated barrel. The bullet would spin down the tube and exit spiraling through the air like a football passed by a quarterback today. These "Pennsylvania long rifles" were accurate at a range of up to 400 yards, but they were more time-consuming to produce and thus more costly. Precision was a must with barrel making, because the ammunition would eventually be fired out of it. Sloppy barrel work would result in a gun that did not shoot straight.

Stocks were made of wood, usually some form of hardwood. The barrel was attached to the stock, with the stock being the part of the gun that the owner held when firing. Creating a stock required a mastery of woodworking that included everything from choosing the right type of wood to cutting and sanding, and then finishing it, which sometimes required carving decorative patterns.

Putting together a gun's lock was particularly delicate work. The lock used parts such as triggers, hammers, matchlocks, flintlocks, pans, and tiny screws and springs. Often a gunsmith had to make each of these parts himself, a process that could take days. Lock crafting also called for error-free work, because a faulty lock could cause serious injuries.

THREE

The Gunsmith's Shop

As with any other tradesman, a gunsmith needed a place to perform his work. He needed a place to hang his tools and store his raw materials. It is important to note, however, that shops and tools dedicated purely to gunsmithing were rare throughout most of the colonial period. Many of these "shops" served other purposes as well.

Location

The typical gunsmith's shop during the colonial era usually was not a retail store like those we have today. The shop was not located on the main street of a busy town among a dozen other shops or part of a shopping center. In the earliest colonial years, the smith's shop was usually a fairly tiny structure located on his own property. If a gunsmith was also a farmer, his smithing shop might be a few hundred feet from his barn. If he was a blacksmith, his gunsmithing tools would be included among all the others, all in the same building. If a jeweler did minor gunsmithing duties for extra money, you might not be able to tell by walking into his place of business. There might be a case full of watches and necklaces, with the gun-repair equipment in a back room, away from the customers' view.

When a person did work solely as a gunsmith, the place where he performed his trade did have some common characteristics. An industrious smith would build a shop on his own property using brick or stone. Large stones could be found in the wilds of most areas, making them free of cost. And because they were fireproof, they were perfect for the hearth that would house the forge the smith would need. The floor was also made from some type of fireproof material, such as clay, gravel, flat stones, or a mixture of these, and eventually they were flattened smooth by years of use. The most basic shop had two main rooms—one for the metalwork, and one for the woodwork. The metalworking room would contain the forge and had adequate ventilation for the smoke and heat.

A Gunsmith's Tools

A gunsmith had to have a wide range of tools at his disposal. However, it is important to note that most of these tools were not exclusive to the gunsmithing trade. Many tools used by a gunsmith were also common to blacksmiths, wood carvers, or jewelers. A few, however, served only the needs of a gunsmith.

One such tool was known as a **boring bench**. The purpose of a boring bench was to bore the hole in the gun's barrel until it was the correct diameter, or caliber. A boring bench was long and narrow, often made from two pieces of heavy timber similar in size and shape to the wood beneath railroad tracks. In the long space between these two pieces was another piece, called a carriage, that could be moved back and forth and set in specific positions. The barrel was securely fastened to this. On one end of the bench was a long rod of metal similar to a drill bit. It was attached to a large wheel that, when cranked, caused the bore to turn. The bore then went into the gun barrel, where it drilled the hole to the proper size. The wheel was sometimes cranked by hand, but other times it was attached to a larger wheel that was powered by moving water, such as in a stream or river, through a waterwheel just outside the shop. The advantage of using water power was that the gunsmith did not have to perform the tiring cranking chore. A wheel turned by water usually had greater strength and speed, too. As a result, a gunsmith could bore more barrels in less time.

Making a gun barrel was a tedious and exacting process. A poorly crafted barrel meant a gun that would not fire straight.

Similar to a boring bench was a **rifling bench**. Its job was to cut a series of spiral grooves into the inside of the barrel. Spiral grooves made a bullet spin as it went through the barrel, which gave it greater accuracy. The barrel was attached to one end of the rifling bench. At the other end was a cylinder with spiral grooves around the outside. A rod was attached at one end to the cylinder, and the other end ran through and out the barrel. At that end was a sharp "tooth" that did the cutting. When the gunsmith gradually pulled back the cylinder, the rod was pulled through the barrel, and the tooth cut a groove as it turned, thus creating a spiral groove inside the barrel. After the first groove was cut, the rod was removed from the cylinder and set back into the barrel for another pass. It would have a different starting point this time, however, and cut a second groove as a result. The most common number of grooves cut in total was around seven.

Another tool, relatively minor but still important, was called a **pan borer**. It was little more than a file that could be attached to a bracket and then turned. Its limited purpose was to carve a depression in the pan of the firing mechanism, which would then be used to hold the gunpowder priming charge. A gunsmith could still create this depression with ordinary hand tools, but the pan borer made the job quicker and easier.

Beyond this short list of specialized tools, a gunsmith also made wide use of many others—those that were common to professions beyond his own. For example, a gunsmith's shop would likely feature woodworking tools like saws, axes, drills and bits, chisels, rasps, floats, and planes, plus a wide variety of blacksmithing tools, such as anvils, hammers, vises, clamps, tongs, irons, pliers, files, shears, bellows, and, of course, the forge itself, which was just as important to a blacksmith as a gunsmith. A lathe was used for polishing, mostly barrels. Screwdrivers of different sizes aided in assembly, and chisels and knives were necessary for decorative carvings and other uses. There are many estate records of gunsmiths showing an impressive collection of tools and other equipment.

Materials

Gunsmiths often had to keep a supply of raw materials handy in order to make whatever weapons their customers required. Generally speaking, these materials were a variety of either metal or wood. Steel and iron were the most common metals, particularly for making barrels. They were inexpensive compared to other metals and fairly easy to work with. Smaller parts such as screws and pins would also be made from one or the other. When available, and when a customer could afford it, copper or brass would be used instead. Engraved plating and similar decoration could be rendered from common metals such as tin, copper, or brass, or precious metals like silver, gold, or platinum.

As for woods, gunsmiths preferred hardwoods over softwoods primarily for their durability, but also because, when finished,

Accessories

Gunsmiths often made additional money selling gun-related accessories, many of which were essential to gun ownership. Gunpowder was one such item. It was a mixture of potassium nitrate and charcoal, with sulfur sometimes also included. When ignited, it produced the required force to fire a gun's ammunition. Gunpowder could be transported with a powder horn—a curved animal horn that was wide at one end (making it easy to fill with powder) and nearly pointed at the other (the actual point would be clipped off so the powder could be conveniently loaded into a weapon in a narrow stream). Among the most commonly used horns were those of buffalo or cattle. They would be capped at either end to hold the powder in place, and a length of string or rope would be attached for ease of carrying.

Another common accessory, of course, was the ammunition itself. This usually came in the

Some gunsmiths also made the accessories that were vital to gun ownership, including ammunition, spare gun parts, and tools for basic gun maintenance.

form of bullets, balls, or lead shot, and varied in size according to intended use. Balls were usually made of lead, but sometimes stone as well. A ramrod was a long, narrow stick that had many purposes. One was to push ammunition down the barrel for loading. Similarly, there was an attachment that could be put on one end to pull balls back out. Another attachment, called a gunworm, had two spiraled points that helped the owner clean the gun by loosening residue in the barrel that had built up from the gunpowder, which was fairly dirty. Spare flints—tiny pieces of metal—were essential to spark and ignite gunpowder. Once a flint wore down and no longer threw a good spark, the gun would fail to fire. Thus, a smart gun owner always carried extras. A few gunsmiths offered bayonets, which were attached to the end of the barrel and basically turned a rifle into a long sword. A few gunsmiths offered carrying cases for their rifles or pistols, as well as bags for ammunition.

they were very attractive. Among the most common woods were maple and walnut, which were relatively easy to acquire in colonial America. Others included beech, cherry, and ash, although these could be expensive. The buyer made the final decision on what would be used, since he was paying for it. A wise gunsmith made a point of keeping bulk quantities of metal and wood on hand. Both could be purchased or traded for, often in the form of discarded furniture or large logs (wood), or unwanted silverware, pots and pans, or candlesticks (metal), which would eventually be melted down in the forge. Large hunks of hardwood could be taken from parcels of land that were being cleared for farming. A smith could cut them into smaller pieces, called blanks, and leave them to dry for as long as five to seven years. He would also keep an ongoing collection of small nails, screws, pins, springs, and other small parts. He never knew when something might be useful.

FOUR

A Day in the Life

Of all the duties of a gunsmith, certainly the most demanding was building a gun from scratch. It required a large investment of time, and much attention to detail. Gunsmiths became busier as America's colonial era drew to a close. Guns were in great demand during the American Revolution, when the governments of Europe had stopped supplying colonists with weapons and ammunition.

Making a Gun

Gunmaking began with the barrel—the part of the gun around which every other part is based. The first step was to take a strip of metal, which was called a **skelp**, and heat the center of it in the forge until it became bendable. The length and thickness of the skelp was determined by the type of gun being made. It was then set on a tool called a **barrel anvil**, which had several grooves on it, each of a different size. It was pounded around a long rod, called a **mandrel**, a little at a time. It was then brought back to the forge, where a different section of the skelp would be heated, and then brought back to the barrel anvil again. Eventually the smith would have a tube, and this was the start of the barrel. If it sounds like this was a lot of work just to create a tube, remember that there were no tools that could simply drill through a solid metal rod in colonial days.

The next step was boring the barrel. To do this, the barrel was set tight upon the boring bench and then run gently but firmly into the drilling bit, which was powered either by a waterwheel or by hand. Precision boring was crucial, because a barrel that had flaws on the inside or was not straight would be unusable. The diameter of the hole that was bored determined the gun's caliber. If a large hole was required, a smith might have to use more than one bit, starting small and getting larger until he got to the right size. The most common test gunsmiths used to determine if the barrel was straight was to run a fine thread through it, then pull the thread tight. If the inside of the barrel did not follow the thread line perfectly, it was tapped with a hammer until it did.

The third step may have been rifling the barrel, unless the

weapon was meant to be a smooth-bore musket. The barrel was attached to the rifling bench, and a rod was run through it. The rod had a tooth on one end, and the other end of the rod was guided by a spiral cylinder. When the rod was pulled through the barrel, it would cut a spiraling groove on the inside of the barrel. This would be done in several different starting positions, thus cutting several grooves inside the barrel.

With the basic construction done, the gunsmith went about making the barrel more presentable. For this, he had to apply the barrel to a large **grindstone**, where all the scuffs, scratches, pits, hammer marks, and other imperfections would be eliminated. The gunsmith might also take the time to polish the barrel to a handsome shine, depending on the demands of the person buying it.

A Bit of Woodworking

Making stocks involved working with wood rather than metal, but was no less challenging. First, there was the issue of size and shape. There was no "standard" stock in colonial times—each one was made according to the directions of the customer. A gunsmith often had pre-made models of several different styles available, but sometimes a customer wanted something a little different.

Once the form of the stock was decided, the gunsmith drew an outline of it onto a wood blank. An experienced smith could tell which areas of a blank were strongest, usually from the direction and tightness of the grain. He also wanted to use grain that had a naturally attractive pattern to it.

After tracing, the stock would be carefully cut. Then the smith would use hand tools to carefully work out the curved channel in the top of the stock where the barrel would sit. He would lightly coat the barrel with chalk or oil, then set it temporarily into this channel. Whatever spots were left behind when the barrel was removed had to be worked down further. After that was done, the gunsmith traced the areas where the lock assembly would go, then carefully cut cavities into the wood to fit each piece. This was painstaking, time-consuming work, and the greatest delicacy was required. An impatient smith could easily cut too deep, cut crookedly, or put a crack in the wood, which then required him to start all over with a new piece.

Once all the holes for the lock pieces

Stocks were made from wood and required experienced hands. One mistake could cause cracks or splits, and the smith would have to start all over again.

were finished, the smith could tend to any decorative work the customer requested. This might include carving out more cavities to make room for inlays, or to render carvings. For the latter, the images would be drawn on and then cut lightly with a sharp blade before deeper carving took place. Due to the tough nature of hardwoods, this decorative step required great patience and just the right combination of force and gentleness.

Very few gunsmiths made their own lock parts. These parts were either imported from Europe or cast in a colonial **foundry**. The few smiths who did make their own used standard designs that could be modified slightly if requested by the buyer, but it was rare for a colonial gunsmith to make fully customized locks. Once he had a full set of lock parts on hand, he could then move on to the final step in the gunmaking process—putting all the pieces together and making sure the gun fired correctly. Then it was ready for presentation to the paying customer.

Maintenance Work

Gunsmiths were often called upon not just to make guns but also to maintain them. Specifically, this meant cleaning and repair. Cleaning required more than just polishing a gun until it looked nice. The barrel had to be free of all grime and soot resulting from prolonged use, as buildup from powder could seriously affect a

From Gunsmith to Factory Manager

As tensions between the colonies and the British government rose and it became clear that war was imminent, colonial leaders often put hefty demands on gunsmiths to increase their production well beyond what was normal for them. As a result, many gunsmiths had to become factory managers as

Intricate decoration on some guns, as seen here, often had to be sacrificed during the American Revolution because smiths had to make large numbers of guns fairly quickly.

well, often overseeing large staffs and occupying much larger buildings than their usual tiny shops. One such smith who found himself in this difficult position was William Henry. Born in Lancaster, Pennsylvania, in 1729, Henry was a gunsmithing apprentice while still in his teens, and by his early twenties he was running his own shop. In March 1776, with the American Revolution in full swing, he received a request from the Pennsylvania government for 200 muskets. He already had a factory up and running at the time but was forced to hire more smiths—some of whom he would later dismiss, possibly for failure to meet quality standards—in order to fulfill the contract. He was also responsible for maintaining and repairing existing weapons of the Revolutionary Army, as well as the production of ammunition.

Sometimes these mass-production factories had to be built from scratch, and a smith had to ask his local government for enough money to get them up and running. He also had to watch carefully to make sure the quality of the guns being produced did not diminish. It was relatively easy to make a gun of fine craftsmanship when the smith was doing just one or two at a time, at a pace with which he was comfortable. But when he had orders to produce ten or twenty a week, there was always the concern that their quality might suffer.

weapon's accuracy. A lock that had accumulated too much filth might not fire properly (or at all). Also, stocks that were not kept clean would deteriorate faster than those that were.

A busy gunsmith might have an apprentice or assistant handle cleaning duties, whereas repair work required greater skill and attention. Among the most common repair jobs was the replacement of stocks. It was certainly cheaper for a gun owner to have a stock replaced than to purchase an entirely new weapon. If a stock became cracked or broken, a competent gunsmith could replace it relatively easily. Sometimes the barrel would come loose from the stock and had to be reattached. If a gun was passed from one owner to another, the new owner might prefer a stock of greater length or width to make the gun more comfortable to use. Repair work also included the replacement of lost or damaged lock parts, as there were many and they often wore out, or the adjustment of sights on the barrel. As tensions between the colonies and Britain increased, the art of keeping guns properly maintained became crucial to the colonies' armies. Thus, the cleaning and repairing of guns became, for many gunsmiths, a booming part of their profession.

FIVE

The Gunsmith and His Community

Gunsmiths were usually regarded in their community as skilled craftsmen. The delicate and highly detailed nature of their work, the rapt attention to detail it required, and the necessary reliability of their products meant that gunsmithing could be successfully performed by only the most sober and talented individuals.

A Man of Necessity

The fact that many smiths were able to work effectively not just in gunsmithing, but in related professions such as whitesmithing, blacksmithing, woodworking, and so on made them all the more respected. Some developed such high reputations that their guns were looked upon not just as firearms but as pieces of art, collectibles of a kind, to be used with great care and passed down through generations.

During the colonial era, ownership of a gun often played a crucial role in one's survival. Thus, the role of a gunsmith in a community was equally important. Colonists needed reliable guns for a variety of reasons. Many people hunted in order to feed themselves and their families. A gun was also crucial in fending off attacks from wild animals that might harm a family, prey on farm animals that were being kept for slaughter or to produce dairy products, or destroy crops. An animal's fur could

The armies of early America relied on gunsmiths not only to make their weapons, but also to keep them in excellent working order.

also be turned into clothing or blankets, and the bones made into a variety of tools and other handy items. Animals hunted with the aid of a gun could also be used for trade, enabling a colonist to acquire a variety of needed products. And during times of war, whether the war was with American Indians or soldiers from overseas, a colonist had little chance without his weapon.

The importance of gunsmithing to a colonial community during times of military conflict was tremendous. Colonial governments urged anyone capable of making a gun to be on call if and when their skills were needed. An example of this is given by author Harold Gill, who wrote *The Gunsmith in Colonial Virginia*: "In 1705, when there was an apparent danger that Virginia might be invaded during Queen Anne's War, the General Assembly allowed militia officers to 'impress' any smith, wheel-wright, carpenter or other artificer, whatsoever . . . for the fixing of arms and making carriages for great guns, or for doing any other work whatsoever, where need shall be of such artificer."

In the Service of His Government

Many of the colonists who served in local militias were required by law to purchase their own guns, but some were so poor that they could not afford them. They were not pleased with the idea of having to use their own money in the first place. Some government officials asked gunsmiths to lower their prices to make their guns more affordable. Even then, some people could not come up with the money to buy a gun. In many areas, local governments eventually gave in and paid to arm their militia. The weapons still had to be maintained properly, however, and they were considered government property.

The American Revolution—and the future of the United States—would have turned out very differently if not for the skilled services of America's gunsmiths.

A smart gunsmith, like any other businessman, went to great pains to keep track of all his spending and earning. He watched and recorded all money that was spent, as well as all money that was made. There were times, however, when a gunsmith had trouble simply getting paid for his work. Accounts carefully kept and then presented before government assemblies were sometimes met with excuses or apologies instead of actual payments. Sometimes smiths were paid in trade, with tobacco or food. Trading for goods and services instead of using cash, known as the barter system, was not at all unusual in colonial times. Still, a gunsmith occasionally found it difficult to maintain his standing when not paid on time, paid only partially, or not paid at all.

The Gunsmith's Legacy

The importance of the gunsmith to the colonial history of the United States is tremendous. Reliable rifles and pistols were often the only tool of protection at a colonist's disposal, the most effective means of protecting the home and family. Guns were also crucial for hunting animals for their meat, bones, and hides. Without the security of a good weapon and the talents of a gunsmith to maintain it, a colonist became vulnerable and had to rely on the mercy of fate. There is little doubt that the battle for North America that became known as the American Revolution was dependent upon guns, either provided by America's French and Dutch allies, or built by their own gunsmiths. Without the talents of the colonial gunsmiths in creating and repairing Revolutionary weapons, there may not have been an independent United States of America.

Capture the Flag

This is a fun warm-weather activity based on a classic game that you can play with a small group of friends.

Capture the Flag is one of the oldest games around. It involves two "sides" trying to capture each other's "flag." In this case, you will use balloons instead of actual flags, and you will have water guns as your "weapons." For safety's sake (and to ensure maximum fun), you should use adequate eye protection, and remember never to shoot your opponents in the face. You should probably also wear bathing suits and T-shirts, and remember to bring along some towels!

You Will Need

- Two balloons filled with water
- Enough water guns for everyone
- Adequate eye protection for everyone (e.g., swimming goggles)
- An outside area where it's okay to get wet (e.g., a backyard or open field in a park)

Steps

1. Set up the balloons on each side of the field.

2. Divide the group into two teams.

3. Each team's objective is to defend their own balloon while trying to burst the balloon of their opponent. When a player is hit by a water gun, he becomes "frozen" for a certain amount of time (say, five seconds).

4. The first team to burst the opponents' balloon wins.

Glossary

American Revolution a period of rebellion by American colonists in an attempt to break free of British rule and establish an independent nation

apprentice one who learns a trade from a more experienced individual, known as a master

barrel the tubular part of a gun through which the ammunition is fired

barrel anvil a tool with multiple grooves upon which a gun barrel was pounded in order to shape it

boring bench a device with a long drill bit designed to make holes in gun barrels

forge furnace in which a gunsmith would heat metals in order to get them soft enough for gunmaking

foundry a place where metals are melted and cast

grindstone a large round stone that, when turned, was used to remove scuffs, scratches, pits, hammer marks, and other imperfections from a gun barrel

guild an organization whose purpose is to ensure a high standard of quality by the workers in a particular trade

indentured servant individuals required to serve an employer for a set period of time

lock mechanism on a gun, made up of many smaller parts, that enables the weapon to fire

mandrel a long rod around which a strip of metal was pounded in order to shape it into a gun barrel

militia	a military force made up of citizens from a local area, usually with minimal training and only used in times of emergency
pan borer	a filing device designed to carve a depression into the pan of a gun's firing mechanism
rifling bench	a device designed to cut spiral grooves inside a gun barrel using a long rod with a sharp tooth at one end
skelp	a "raw" strip of metal intended for use in gunmaking
stock	part of a gun upon which the lock and barrel are attached, and where the weapon is held by its user
whitesmith	an artisan who works with metals, most notably tin and some forms of iron

Find Out More

BOOKS

Hazen, Walter. *Colonial Times.* Tucson, AZ: Good Year Books, 2008.

Johnson, Terry (compiler). *What Really Happened in Colonial Times.* Mississauga, ON: Knowledge Quest Books, 2007.

Kalman, Bobby. *A Visual Dictionary of a Colonial Community.* New York: Crabtree Publishing, 2008.

Roberts, Russell. *Life in Colonial America.* Hockessin, DE: Mitchell Lane Publishers, 2007.

WEBSITES

Colonial Life in Early America

http://www.kidinfo.com/American_History/Colonization_Colonial_Life.html

Kid Info page on colonial life, featuring many excellent links and loads of useful information.

Colonial Times in America

http://www.socialstudiesforkids.com/subjects/colonialtimes.htm

The Social Studies for Kids page on the life and times of colonial America has many excellent links.

Colonial Williamsburg for Kids: Games and Activities

http://www.history.org/kids/games/

The games and activities page from the Colonial Williamsburg site has many fun and interesting things to do, all with educational value.

Index

Page numbers in **boldface** are illustrations.

About the Author

Wil Mara is the award-winning author of more than 120 books, many of which are educational titles for young readers. More information about his work can be found at www.wilmara.com.